When Autumn Leaves Start to Fall

by Judy Condon

©2015 Marsh Homestead Country Antiques, LLC

Library of Congress Cataloging-in-Publications Data
When Autumn Starts to Fall by Judy Condon
ISBN 978-0-9912026-8-3

Oceanic Graphic Printing, Inc.
105 Main Street
Hackensack, NJ 07601

Printed in China

Layout and Design by Pat Lucas,
   lucasketch_design@yahoo.com
   pat-lucas.fineartamerica.com
Edited by Trent Michaels

Table of Contents

About the Author

Judy Condon is a native New Englander, which is evident in her decorating style and the type of antiques she collects and sells. Her real passion is 19thC authentic dry red or blue painted pieces. While Judy enjoyed a professional career as a teacher, Principal, and Superintendent of Schools in Connecticut, Judy's weekends were spent at her antique shop, *Marsh Homestead Country Antiques*, located in Litchfield, Connecticut.

When her husband, Jeff, was relocated to Virginia, Judy accepted an early retirement from education and concentrated her energy and passion for antiques into a fulltime business. Judy maintains a website, *www.marshhomesteadantiques.com* and has been a Power Seller on eBay® for 15 years under the name "superct".

Judy and her husband Jeff returned four years ago to their roots in New England and have completed renovating a 19thC cape in Massachusetts. The house was featured in her early 2012 book *Back Home-Simply Country* which included many before and after pictures. Judy has five children and seven grandchildren and enjoys reading, golf, bridge, tennis, and volunteering in the educational system in St Maarten. Judy does her best to provide teaching materials and children's books to the schools in St. Maarten with the hope of helping establish classroom libraries.

Judy's first 35 books in the "simply country" series have been instant hits and some are in their second and third printing. Sample pages from each book and the availability can be viewed at her website.

Judy continues to write what has become known as 'the simply country' book series and is currently working on four books for 2016 including a second educational book co-authored with Sherry D. Pees titled *A Primer for a Country Dwelling*. Recently Judy deviated briefly from the series to write *Nothing Tastes as Good as Skinny*, a tough-love approach and Program for weight loss and weight loss management. As the subtitle indicates, 'this ain't no diet book'! Awareness for the book has been made with a number of editorials in national magazines. Judy maintains a Facebook page and website for the book at *www.asgoodasskinny.com*

Her books are available on her website at *www.marshhomesteadantiques.com*, from Amazon.com, through her email at *marshhomestead@comcast.net* or *marshhomestead@gmail.com* or by phone at 877-381-6682. Judy also maintains a Facebook page *Marsh Homestead Country Antiques*.

Introduction

What is it about autumn that brings out the best of us who love to decorate country? It's been a year since my book *When Summer Turns to Autumn* was offered and sold out in two weeks! I'm still asking myself what was it that made that book so popular? I've learned from many readers that they love autumn for decorating – almost as much as getting their home spruced up for the holidays! We have such a wealth of drieds available to us – corn husks, Yarrow, Sweet Annie and of course our favorite – bittersweet.

Someone commented that we need the varieties of seasons to be able to appreciate the uniqueness of each. While inside we may be decorating with muted tones of dried naturals, outside our windows the world is alive with color that we capture and hold dear in our memory to carry us through the darker days of winter. While we begin to 'power down' from summer vacations and the brightness of a hot summer sun, we think football, school buses, cinnamon sticks, apples, chilly mornings, wooded paths of fallen leaves, pumpkin pies, and a time to gather not only our harvests but our families to give thanks. One poet described it as a grand finale for the year while Albert Camus called autumn 'a second spring when every leaf is a flower'. It's the season where we can transition into shorter hours of daylight and earlier dusk; a time to enjoy the cooler evenings, the first fire of the season and a warm bowl of homemade soup or stew! You will love the recipe shared by Lisa Jenks for 'Pumpkin Stew' on page 67.

Autumn . . . when poplar and maple leaves make the trees appear as torches while fruit trees lose leaves but are transformed with the color of the fruit they bear. In my gardens, I am gathering the numerous country accents I displayed in the beds the previous spring to be stored in the barn until April, filling the birdfeeder more regularly so those of my feathered friends who will 'stay around' can begin their preparation for winter and placing leaves in my garden beds so that with the help of winter snows the soil may be enriched.

Once I've added the gourds to the large trencher on my table, changed out the door piece on the front door and added bittersweet vines in numerous spots, I'm ready for shorter days, longer books, fireside warmth and flannel sheets. And how ironic that during the season of transformation and the crowning glory of the year, I can look around with a sense of inner quiet and peace – appreciative for all my blessings with time to pause and give thanks.

Chapter 1

Paul and Allison Bertinotti

Sometimes even the practicality of moving to a different home for additional space is outweighed by the charm of the place where we currently live. Such is the case with Paul and Allison Bertinotti of Evansville, Indiana. While their family has started to outgrow the space, neither Paul nor Allison is willing to forfeit the character and charm of the 1938 brick house they have called home for the past 18 years. As a compromise, Allison revealed they might add on at some point and would rather do that than move. Further, the location is ideal for Paul's occupation as an ironworker and Allison enjoys the luxury of providing child care for a friend allowing her to be an at home mom.

Allison chuckled as she confessed that when she left home, she was never going to decorate as her mother had. However after a while, Allison purchased her first antique and over the years has gravitated towards a more primitive look as so many of us have. Paul is not as enthusiastic about the style but has learned to appreciate Allison's talent in decorating and feels a sense of pride when visitors show appreciation for the look and feel of their home. Allison particularly enjoys it when her teenager's friends visit and remark that it's 'cool'.

Allison keeps the rooms simply trimmed with a paint from Valspar called 'Colonial Beige' throughout giving continuity to the house.

The small worktable which Allison uses as a coffee table holds a deck of playing cards once belonging to her grandmother and which she found in an old trunk her mother passed on to her.

Allison's daughter created the unique centerpiece on the mantel by placing a miniature pumpkin on top of each of three hog scrapers. The corn husk wreath provides a focal point above. A set of graduated manganese jugs is arranged on the right side of the mantel while the opposite end holds a crafted Halloween plate made by folk artist Becky Geis of Heart of Newburgh, a local shop.

Allison had the good fortune a number of years ago to purchase an item on eBay© and discover that the seller lived in the same town and was willing to drop it off to save shipping costs. Since then Allison and Judy Bailey have been fast friends. Judy's home was featured in the previous holiday book Sleigh Bells Ring. Not only does Judy have an eye for country decorating, she has provided Allison with great ideas and new acquisitions as Judy sells as well as collects antiques. The hanging candleholder was a gift to Allison from Judy.

The exquisite settle in the corner was the first substantial antique Allison purchased. The patina is superb on the back and the blue painted base striking. Allison found the small box at a neighbor's yard sale and saw it immediately as a wall shelf. Corn husks glued on top of a pumpkin was an idea she found on Pinterest. The wooly stick-legged sheep belonged to Allison's grandmother.

Paul and Allison made the pair of make-do chairs on either side of the reproduction cabinet which holds a television. A Family Heirloom Weavers remnant hangs over the back of one of the chairs. Paul is an avid gardener and grew many of the herbs drying on the vintage rack in the corner.

    Allison finds many of her antique pewter pieces on eBay© and at flea markets; the built-in cabinet to the left of the front door holds some of the collection.

    The back door leads to the kitchen and dining nook through a screened porch. The archway opens to a cozy dining room where Allison used an old fireplace mantel with a similar color original paint as the trim paint in the house.

She repurposed an early grain scoop as a candleholder. At the far left, Allison utilized a small peg rack to display textiles and added a cluster of dried sunflowers to off-set the muted colors in the grouping.

Paul measured and drew the squares on the hardwood floors and Allison painted them with mustard and black squares to replicate a floor cloth. A coat of polyurethane on top protects the paint. An early soap box, marked 'Ideal Soap', becomes a wall shelf which Allison filled with old bottles, a gourd and a fabric-covered book.

Allison purchased all of the bonnets on eBay© from Judy Bailey which was the catalyst for their initial meeting.

The wall clock was a gift from Allison's mother; the sugar cone was purchased on eBay©.

Allison painted the floor in the kitchen using the same process as she and Paul had used in the dining room. The wonderful sawbuck table was purchased from Judy Bailey and it's perfect for the size of the kitchen.

Three shelves above not only provide display space for collectibles such as tinware but also give their kitchen the feeling of a pantry! The blue green tin cake box belonged to Allison's grandmother. Allison purchased the vintage laundry tub from a friend and found it fit perfectly in the corner. The small cupboard above is a reproduction.

The linens on the master bedroom bed are from Family Heirloom Weavers.

The bed table is comprised of two trunks; the bottom one belonged to Allison's grandmother and was filled with vintage treasures when Allison was gifted it. The top trunk was purchased at a local antique shop. The child's chair and doll were gifts to Allison from her mother.

Judy Bailey made the fabric-covered boxes standing on the chest.

She also made the shower curtain in the bathroom from feed sacks stamped 'Bemis'.

The screened back porch is one of the charming features of the home for Allison. The round table and chairs were purchased at a local antique shop.

Although Allison has been limited by the space in their home, she gives credence to her philosophy that if you take your time, choose wisely and are not afraid of trial and error, it's possible to create a warm and welcoming home no matter how large or small the space.

Chapter 2

John and Ann Davis

Six years ago, John and Ann Davis were fortunate to find a new log home which was partially built but had been left unfinished on the inside. It took them six months before they were able to move into their new home but during that time they were able to finish the interior to their liking. The log home sits on two-and-a-half acres in St. Marys, West Virginia – a small community along the southern Ohio border. In fact, they are close enough to Ohio that Ann makes frequent trips to shops there as she has better luck finding antique treasures in Ohio than anywhere else.

John and Ann live with their 18-year-old granddaughter Emily who has caught the country decorating bug and helps Ann decorate for the various seasons. In fact, it was Emily who did most of the exterior arranging of the autumn decorations.

John works at a chemical plant nearby and over the years has come to appreciate Ann's style of decorating. Ann admits he now brings her home things he finds in his travels and brought Ann home one of the grinding wheels pictured above.

Ann grew up on a farmhouse and has always liked the style. When she and John were first married, she started buying small pieces. The first real purchase early on was a small spinning wheel and she attributes that piece to starting the trend. She is becoming more primitive with time but admits that she has to mix styles as comfort, as well as style, is a concern.

The large front porch is ideal for larger primitives such as the barrel in the corner which holds a primitive folk art barn and the early wash tub.

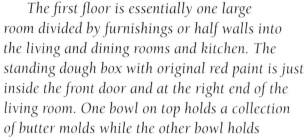

The first floor is essentially one large room divided by furnishings or half walls into the living and dining rooms and kitchen. The standing dough box with original red paint is just inside the front door and at the right end of the living room. One bowl on top holds a collection of butter molds while the other bowl holds miniature gourds. The textiles above are a mix of old and new; the shoes are early.

John and Ann have designated replacing the wall to wall carpeting in the living room with wooden floors as their next major project.

Ann loves to collect rocking horses and the white horse on the wall is one of three early horses she displays in the room.

The large cupboard in the back corner retains its original green paint and is pegged construction. An assortment of early quilts fills the shelves.

One of Ann's favorite pieces is the immigrant baby cradle which is initialed and dated 1809.

Ann painted the old cobbler's bench black to match the black and mustard fabric of the couch.

John received the grandfather's clock in the corner from his employer upon completion of 25 years of service.

Ann found the dry sink with attic surface at an antique shop in Ohio. Above, a sieve holds small pumpkins and a fabric crow; above that is a silhouette of scarecrows. The hooked rug of the pumpkin below was done by Julie Butler.

An early trencher with red paint sits on the center of the Amish-made table and chairs.

A large late 19thC stepback in the corner is filled with measures, firkins and buckets. An old grain sieve stands on top.

Ann used an old apple ladder to display some of her basket collection.

The kitchen is behind the diningroom. The cabinets are buttermilk painted oak. Standing on the counter is a large Enterprise coffee grinder purchased in Illinois and purportedly from an old general store. The shelf on the wall holds five early coffee grinders and vintage tin containers.

The pie screen keeps the flies off the faux biscuits! The winnowing board is old as is the treen bowl in which Ann has placed some faux crackers.

The oak Possum Belly Hoosier was found at a local shop – it dates to the early 20thC and is perfect for holding jars, treen bowls and measures. The bowls on the bottom shelf hold cookie cutters – another of Ann's passions!

The old Aunt Jemima cookie jar was purchased from Jimmy Rochelle of Homestead Primitives in Tennessee.

John built the guestroom bed with pre-cut logs. Authentic Amish clothing hangs on a peg rack over the head of the bed.

Ann says she is never at a loss for projects. In fact, the back room she said is filled with furniture ready to repair or refinish. When not refurbishing, she is on the hunt at yard sales, garage sales and flea markets. She and John often just travel back country roads and are amazed at the treasures they've come across. Ann admits it takes some patience to upgrade from the earlier pieces she once furnished their home with, but the wait has been worth it as she enjoys it all!

Chapter 3

❖ ⊛ ❖

Christine Mulhearn

When I first pulled up in front of Christine Mulhearn's home in Worcester, Massachusetts I knew immediately that I was at the right house by all the wonderful fall decorations in the yard. However what surprised me a bit and caused me to pause was the fact that Christine had told me she had a daycare center in her home and I thought this small house couldn't accommodate six young children too. I was wrong! Not only does the house accommodate six well-behaved children, it is full of country décor and the children moved through the house without disturbing anything.

Christine has lived in her 1970's home for 25 years and has had a daycare center there for 24 years. While the living space in the house consists of 720 square feet, Christine remodeled the basement and uses that additional 720 square footage the majority of the time for the children.

Christine admits she is often frustrated by the size of the house but has also managed to maximize the space using the front porch, side deck and even a part of the backyard.

Christine decorates primarily with reproduction pieces and loves to refinish unsalvageable older pieces. The ladderback chair in the living room belonged to Christine's mother.

The new mantel has been accessorized with a small heater to replicate a fireplace. Christine purchased the bowl rack at Primitive Thymes in Spencer, Massachusetts.

Christine's brother-in-law built the shelf alongside the stairwell to the basement. The shelf holds a collection of bears – many of which are Boyd's.

Christine had the dry sink and cupboard hanging above made and then refinished both pieces herself. She used mustard paint, her favorite color, and then applied a dark walnut stain to give the pieces an aged appearance. Sanding them in spots further enhanced the look.

The trencher on the bench under the window dates to the late 1700s and was a gift from Christine's sister Patricia Ram, who has been a major influence in Christine's decorating. Patricia's home is First Period and was featured in a previous book, The Joy of Country. A shelf over the window is filled with stoneware crocks Christine found at the Salvation Army!

The kitchen table is 19thC and was purchased from Craig's list. The ladderback chairs are new. The apothecary on the counter was purchased at Village Primitives, a shop in nearby Sturbridge.

The countertops are laminate. The window treatments are linen.

The small two-drawer box on the winnowing board covering the stove was another Salvation Army find.

Christine has collected yellowware and banded bowls for years, many of which she found at the Brimfield Shows.

The piggin bucket beside the door, shown

right, is old and was found at Bernat Mill Antiques in Uxbridge, Massachusetts. Christine found the high chair below at The Walker Homestead Show in Brookfield, Massachusetts

The master bedroom bed, shown on page 27, is covered with a Family Heirloom Weaver's spread. The spinning wheel at the foot of the bed is engraved 1865 while the bonnets are newly-made textiles. A lamp sits on top of a graduated set of early chests with original paint.

Christine refinished the tall cupboard and smaller cabinet using the same process as on the living room pieces.

The rope bed in Christine's son's room was purchased from her sister. It has the original red paint and dates to the late 18thC. The settle beside it was a purchase from The Bernat Mill Antiques group shop. Christine found the large wall apothecary hanging above the settle on Craig's list and refinished it.

When Christine isn't caretaking toddlers, refinishing furniture or antiquing, she enjoys doing punch needlecrafts. The potting shed in the backyard and small deck off the side provide her a place for more vignettes much to the delight of the little ones who wander through Christine's yard and house in wonderment with eyes as big as saucers! Can you imagine what they think of it all when Christine decorates for Christmas?

Chapter 4

❧ ✿ ☙

David and Lana Testa

Iᵗ's always fun to go back and revisit a home during a different season because those of us who can't get enough of rearranging, upgrading and seasonally adding to our country décor, change our rooms on a regular basis – oftentimes to the extent of being unrecognizable. Lana Testa is one such country decorator!

David and Lana Testa's home in Mashpee, Massachusetts was featured in my previous holiday book, *Stockings Were Hung.* At the time David and Lana had just finished moving to six homes in five years and they had recently completed what David deems their last move to Mashpee. When I featured their home in the holiday book, David and Lana had not had time to complete modifications or renovations but in two brief years, major changes have occurred.

David is a retired police officer with the Milford, Massachusetts Police Department while Lana, whose name is familiar to many readers from Facebook, creates original handmade timeworn seasonal figures and sells wholesale through shows, online and reputation. The name of Lana's business is *Winterberry Primitives,* so named from Winterberry Lane where she and David lived in 2009 when Lana started the business.

Lana enjoys accenting her décor with dried naturals using antique pieces as a backdrop. She likes to utilize all available space in a tasteful way and is conscious of mixing textures and color.

The hand-painted sign on the porch speaks to David's position! The blue bench on the porch was made by their youngest son but David and Lana moved to Florida before he had finished the piece. He waited five years until they moved back to present it as a gift.

Lana made the door piece using a bag of fresh apples, rusty wire and some fresh bittersweet.

The trim paint in the Keeping Room is called 'Pumpkin' from The Seraph while the walls are painted 'Lancaster Whitewash' from Benjamin Moore's Historic Collection. The bowl rack was made by David and Lana's son and Lana's dad many years ago. It holds both new and old bowls.

A hand-hammered black iron plate made by Kathy Nugent is the focal point on the mantel and provides contrast for the white pumpkin. Lana made the garland seen across the lintel using faux crab apples that she pinched and squeezed then aged with paint and cinnamon until they looked like dried apples.

A large reproduction mustard painted basket holds a wonderful collection of fall pumpkins, bittersweet and corn husks. The shelf beside the front door holds a collection of redware from Pied Piper.

Lana made the fabric doll named 'Hester' in the corner. The small corner cabinet holds some of the many pieces of yellowware Lana collects.

The upholstered chair is from The Seraph. The linen tobacco panels are from Family Heirloom Weavers.

Lana utilizes the beams in the Gathering Room to display baskets. The trim paint and paneled wall are painted 'Ashley Grey' from Benjamin Moore. Lana purchased the large sawbuck table at a Nan Gurley Antique show. David made the floorcloth beneath it. The high windows in the room not only allow privacy but allow additional display space in the room.

The large antique cupboard is from Molly Garland. The tin candlelight on the table was made by The Tin Peddlar.

David made the spoon rack. The old wooden sink Lana uses as a trencher on the center of the table was another purchase from a Nan Gurley Show.

David made the shelf and the reproduction treen plates which blend well with the old bowl and dry cutting board. The hand-poured blackened wax Luminara candle is from Marsh Homestead Country Antiques.

The large reproduction mustard cupboard in the corner holds a television. The small hutch chair was purchased at the former Jackie's Primitives shop.

Sitting on top of an early gray painted jelly cupboard, Lana filled a square-nailed old red painted box with bittersweet, gourds and a fabric crow she made.

Lana has collected yellowware for years and has displayed many pieces in an antique cupboard she purchased at Jackie's Primitives.

David made the large counterbox to hold various items. It is used frequently and serves a double purpose by blocking the work area from view to those sitting at the other side of the counter.

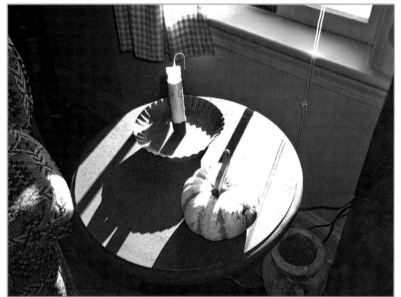

David made the faux fireplace in the master bedroom using an antique door as the back wall. The upholstered chair and stool are from The Seraph. Lana purchased the antique Windsor for $25 and then painted it in layers aging it to look like original black over red. The small candlestick table was purchased at Home Goods and then painted by Lana in the same way she finished the Windsor.

David made the mustard over brown wall cupboard which conceals a flat screen TV in the master bedroom. The dresser below belonged to Lana's mother and Lana painted it a grungy drab brown over mustard.

Lana can be reached through her website, www.picturetrail.com/winterberryprimitives or on Facebook. Her email is winterberryprimz@aol.com.

Chapter 5

Vernon and April Santee

For the past 20 years Vernon and April Santee have been adding, adjusting, and changing what started out to be their early 1960s trailer in Grant Town, West Virginia. In fact, April confessed that with each of the numerous additions over the years, each room became some other kind of room during the process. Essentially, Vernon and April pushed out from each side to add bedrooms, a foyer and a dining room. When they started the process and up until the past 4 to 5 years, April liked country blues and burgundy tones with a few stars thrown in for good measure. She thinks she always had the eye for primitives but it just took her a bit of time 'to get there'. Vernon on the other hand grew up on a farm and has adapted without any difficulty to April's emerging new style of décor. Vernon used to bring home pieces before April was into primitives and she would often not have the slightest idea of what to do with Vernon's finds!

Vernon works in the local grocery store as a meat manager while April has the good fortune to operate her own storage business which allows her to work from their home. April readily admitted that Vernon makes a lot of it happen with their finds as his talent is often utilized to salvage one of April's fresh treasures.

The original trailer is sided with knotty pine from Lowe's and is painted a custom sage green. Vernon made the large wagon in front of the porch as well as the primitive wheelbarrow pictured above. Because the original trailer door was narrower than a standard opening, Vernon crafted a new front screen door.

April leans towards a simpler look which is one reason the bench Vernon made with straight lines holds a place of honor beside the front door.

Vernon also made the tall weathered corner cupboard which April decorates seasonally. The old barn wood is durable and removes any guilt April feels about putting it outside.

A large basket stands on the shelf over the couch in the living room. In keeping with April's preference for simplification, the walls are painted with muted colors throughout and she prefers the drab tones of browns, creams and tans. On either side of the basket are a few of the many barrels and nail kegs April can't seem to pass up. When she and Vernon are taking their boys to their various sporting events, they often pass by shops or flea markets where some of their favorite pieces have been found. April also finds that while 95% of what she sees in a large antique mall are things which hold little interest, she often manages to find one or two pieces tucked in a back corner that she can't live without.

A small primitive table with attic surface holds a dough bowl of bittersweet and gourds. Behind stands a large sieve and nail keg. The black ladderback chair is one of several April inherited from her great-grandmother.

The pie safe with chippy white painted tins caught April's eye in Sweet Memories, a local antique mall in Fairmont, West Virginia. It provides additional much-needed storage in the dining room. The basket on top is filled with dried sunflowers which are passed on to April by her neighbor once the birds have finished with them. A trencher leaning beside the pie safe was purchased at The Craft Connection in Fairmont and is too large for a table but fits perfectly tucked in the side.

April had been intrigued by the table in her mom and dad's garage which her father was using as a worktable. They passed it along to her and she immediately removed three layers of paint and the plywood nailed on top to reveal a lovely early two-board top.

Dried bittersweet fills the slatted wooden carrier which sits on a shelf April has repurposed into a table riser.

April found the long table with cross board base locally. Vernon cut the legs down and scraped off layers of paint. April then rubbed the wood with steel wool and vinegar to give it a worn appearance.

Vernon built the primitive bench as well as the hanging cupboard above which houses some of April's crock collection.

The dining room is at the central part of the house with many rooms leading off of it. A cupboard in the back is located at the edge of the kitchen area.

Vernon and April found the cupboard in a remote location in the mountains.

The elderly man who owned it was in the process of sanding it down and 'updating' it when April and Vernon told him they would take it just the way it was. Removing the glass doors gave space for early wooden buckets and a more primitive look; the top is ideal for another large-handled trencher filled with gourds and dried bittersweet vines.

April painted the kitchen cupboards with Lowe's 'Sturdy Brown'; the countertops are laminate and were purchased at a local hardware store.

A large white pumpkin sits in a dough bowl atop the stool on the island. April stains her white pumpkins with boiled walnut hulls to give the pumpkins a more primitive look.

The slant top box is the ideal size for the windowsill over the sink.

April refers to the small room off the kitchen as the refrigerator room. It allows April to keep small appliances such as a microwave out of view. It also of course provides more space for decorating with buckets filled with rolling pins, nail kegs or barrels.

The illuminated light on top of the open corner cupboard is the focal point in a display of buckets, baskets and crocks. A cluster of gourds is nestled in a sieve on top.

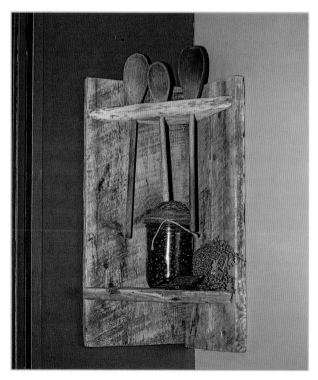

April carried the monochromatic tones into the master bedroom with the same soft tan. The white iron bed belonged to April's great-grandmother and is a piece April had admired since she was a young girl. The patchwork quilt was found at Dad's Primitive Workbench in Ohio.

April uses the 'chippy' white painted cupboard to store clothes. The large gathering basket on top serves the same purpose. With storage space at a premium, the standing trunk serves a dual purpose as a bedtable and storage for more clothing.

April prides herself for her patience to have created the home she has always wanted. She has learned that she doesn't need to fill every spot and if she sees something and keeps going back to it, she had better buy it. Because space is limited, April has learned that the country accessories she purchases, while decorative, must also be functional. She concedes that you can't decorate a home in a week and acknowledges that she is so pleased with the end result of their work, it was worth the wait.

Chapter 6

✦ ✳ ✦

Craig and Andrea Holcomb

Craig and Andrea Holcomb have lived in their Bickmore, West Virginia home for 10 years and its remote location on the side of a big mountain suits them both just fine. They don't even need to be on a bus line as Andrea home schools their two children ages 10 and 14 with Craig's assistance on major projects. Actually Andrea shared that Craig gets to do math and most of the 'fun stuff' while she has to be the taskmaster. Andrea and Craig opted to home school their children when Craig was working long hours as a coal miner and saw too little of the children. Just recently Craig was laid off from his job and he and Andrea are in the process of opening a new door – purchasing a local hardware business.

Andrea decorates and coordinates weddings, is a Mary Kay Rep but also enjoys crafting, photography, gardening and reading. But she said they are an 'outdoors' family and spend much of their time camping, hiking and hunting.

Andrea has always lived with country decorating as her mother owns a shop, *Homestead Primitives*, in nearby Clay, West Virginia. Andrea remembers as a young child admiring the early crocks at her grandmother's home and the spinning wheel her grandmother owned. She remembers seeing her grandparents rocking on the bench which now sits beside the front door of Craig and Andrea's home.

The weathered gate leaning against the front of the house came from Andrea's great-grandfather's farm; it opened to the area where he grew grapes.

The lantern on the small bench belonged to Craig's grandparents.

Andrea is gravitating towards a more colonial decorating style and moving away from the rustic primitives she used to collect. She now prefers the cleaner and simpler look, but still has a few primitive pieces, such as the six-board chest with attic surface, incorporated into the décor.

The charcoal portrait on the mantel causes Craig to ask, "Why can't we have cute pictures of the kids on the mantel instead of a scary woman we don't know?" Andrea admitted the cute pictures are elsewhere in the house and the portrait blends with the overall décor! Andrea collects early pewter which looks lovely with the colors of fall pumpkins. The rifle over the mantel was a gift to Craig from his uncle, a gunsmith.

Andrea had to have the walking wheel when she found it as it reminded her of her grandmother. Baskets are one of Andrea's favorite collectibles and she places them judiciously around the house.

Andrea made all the framed stitched pieces hanging over the couch.

She also stitched the framed piece on the first shelf of the hanging cupboard.

Andrea purchased the corner cupboard from her sister-in-law. It has two three-paneled doors which Andrea liked and many layers of paint. The child's rocking horse atop the early box is old as is the coverlet draped over the rocking chair.

The table and chairs in the dining room are reproductions but the bowback Windsor beside the tall black cupboard is old.

Andrea believes the tall stepback is a married piece which has one board removed on the back as there are rough saw marks on the vertical boards.

Andrea filled an early tool carrier with gourds, corn husks and bittersweet vines. The bottom shelves of the cupboard store early treen bowls.

A dated 1816 sampler, found at a yard sale, and an old coverlet are draped over the settle at one side of the table.

When Craig and Andrea left their first home, Andrea wanted a remembrance and took an old closet door from the house. Andrea's dad built the chimney cupboard seen above right, with lumber sawn from an old walnut tree in the yard.

The small goat cart in front has remnants of blue paint and holds a pair of pumpkins grown by Craig and Andrea's two children.

The patina on the early pie safe is rich making it one of Andrea's favorite antiques in the house. A reproduction wall shelf above holds newly crafted redware.

Tucked in the corner, a small worktable once belonged to Craig's grandparents. It was used in a workshop and when Andrea attempted to clean off the dirt, much of the mustard paint came off as well. However, being a family piece, it is still treasured. Andrea found the bowback Windsor chair at a local antique shop.

The kitchen cabinets are painted with a Lowe's paint called 'Oatmeal'. The floor is tiled and the countertops are laminate.

Craig and Andrea removed a row of suspended cabinets over the cook top to open up the room and create a dining area into the room. The weathered primitive cupboard in the corner appears to be a married piece with the bottom having been a washstand at some point.

Andrea placed a few pieces of redware amidst more of her pewter collection and butter molds. A small butter churn stands on the bottom shelf.

In the opposite corner of the room, the large stoneware crock belonged to Craig's grandparents. It holds a basket of dried corn husks.

Andrea made the window treatments which at first were a startling change from the primitive linens she used to have. She admits they did bring forth a few comments from her primitive friends but she now appreciates how they blend better with the colonial décor than the previous linens! The large window over the sink is simply dressed with baskets which hang from an early rack perhaps once used as a drying rack for herbs.

Andrea attached a small early box to the wall and repurposed it as a cupboard. An old wooden bucket stands on top while the small box on the counter below holds more fall naturals.

Andrea and Craig both enjoy the history connected with many of their antiques. They often travel to the Shenandoah Valley area in Virginia to camp and in their travels have visited Civil War sites. While there are antiques in the house, Craig and Andrea both want their home to be a place which is comfortable and where the children don't have to be afraid they will break something valuable. What is most important to Andrea is that their home is not a museum but rather a place that it is warm and welcoming.

Chapter 7

Leon and Lisa Jenks

Leon and Lisa Jenks have lived in their 1984 New Salem, Massachusetts home for 18 years but it looks nothing like it did when they moved in. Over the years, Leon, a professional landscaper, has cleared the land and established manicured lawns and gardens. An addition in 2009 gave them a family room, additional bedrooms for their five children and a sweeping porch for Lisa to decorate.

Lisa operated a child daycare center in their home for 12 years but closed it when their now 8-year-old son went off to school. Lisa is grateful that she can be a 'stay at home mom' but there is no sitting still! Lisa does the accounting for Leon's business and 'in her spare time', has made almost every piece of furniture in the house! She sloughs it off as 'no big deal' and claims 'everything I know I learned from Leon who is a talented woodworker'. One day, Lisa asked Leon to move his trailer and tools near the backyard pool where she acted as a lifeguard. She decided to begin building furniture, and she 'just did it'! She's been building ever since!

During the time Lisa was providing child daycare, one of the parents invited her to their 1830s cape and Lisa was sold! She came home and began to transform her home.

Lisa chose ACE paint called 'Butterscotch Candy' for the porch color and 'Custard Cream' for the trim. The table in the corner came in handy for providing children with snacks and keeping their wet feet out of the house.

The farm table with blue painted base was the former dining room table. Since it was only about 30 years old, Lisa felt no remorse in painting it blue and added an old door on top to give it a more primitive look. She made the benches from old wood.

Lisa found the buggy seat at Homestead Primitives in Fitchburg, Massachusetts, where she purchases many of the few pieces she doesn't make.

The cushioned bench under the windows was repurposed by Lisa using an outgrown bed belonging to one of the children.

Lisa found the church pew at Haley's Antiques in Athol, Massachusetts and uses the wall above to display a railroad lantern, galvanized tin tub and primitive signs.

The walls of the family room addition are painted with Benjamin Moore 'Acorn Squash'. Lisa wanted to break up the plastered walls of the room with horizontal boards on the base. The boards create not only a different surface but using the boards horizontally versus vertically was more cost effective.

The upholstered furniture is Johnston-Benchworks. The 19thC six-board chest as well as the hooked rug of pineapples on top were found at The Country Mischief in nearby Templeton.

Lisa made the shelf and the dry sink pictured right. A collection of vintage tin candlemolds stands on the shelf below a hooked rug she also made.

Leon made the large black cupboard before Lisa took over! Seen hanging above are a few of Leon's collection of vintage oil cans.

Lisa and Leon put the tile floor down themselves – a messy job Lisa said she would never do again but she likes the outcome! Lisa made the wood box.

Lisa 'inherited' her 14 year old son's vintage lantern collection and was thrilled! She is willing to give them back if he asks but for now, enjoys displaying them around the room.

Lisa built the black shelf which holds many pieces of old pewter. The dowels in the center are ideal for holding pewter plates.

The side table was constructed by Lisa using an early box for which she built a lid and legs. Her intent was to create a piece resembling a standing dough box in red which she had been unable to find! I think she succeeded. Lisa purchased the reproduction tavern sign because it featured a pewter coffee pot and mug blending well with the pieces on the shelf.

One step up from the family room takes a visitor into the dining room and kitchen area where there is so much to see it is breathtaking! Lisa made the farmtable with an old door. On the top, a large box holds a collection of drieds – sunflowers, corn cobs, and artichokes. The runner is from Family Heirloom Weavers.

Lisa built the blue dry sink after seeing the antique one on the cover of my previous book, *The Place We Call Home*. *The mustard shelf above, found at* Homestead Primitives, *holds vintage tinware. The hanging cupboard is early and was purchased at* The Country Mischief.

A children's high chair holds a dough bowl filled with early whisk brooms.

Leon built the large stepback which Lisa immediately painted black; however, after moving it into the room, it was too stark and she over painted it with Old Village 'Antique Pewter'. As her decorating style evolved over the next few years, she again painted it black, leaving the back of the shelves 'Antique Pewter' and loves the look. The piece holds stoneware crocks, measures, mortars and pestles and wooden bowls. In the off season, Lisa uses artificial bittersweet until the real thing is available. She loves the look of fall and keeps her home decorated for her preferred season year round.

Lisa found the slant-top desk at Village
Green in Barre, Massachusetts. She uses it for
her accounting work for Leon's business and not
only likes how it fits into the décor of the room,
but allows her to do her paperwork in the 'hub'
of the house. A vintage gameboard, sometimes
referred to as a hunt board, holds a lantern and
early textiles.

Leon and Lisa scaled down the large original
island in the center of the kitchen and painted
it 'Acorn Squash'. The stacked stools at the
end keep people from hitting their head on the
hanging light above.

Lisa enclosed the refrigerator with beadboard
quickly before Leon returned home from work
as she suspected he might put the brakes on that
project! Notice the unique way Lisa conceals the
ice maker!

The board over the island conceals the original track for the lighting. Lisa adapted a 'cutesy' hanging light decorated with black roosters into a combined chandelier and display for graniteware. She replaced the white candle sleeves with ones covered with fake melted wax then dressed the light with bittersweet.

Lisa sanded down the drop leaf table found in Vermont and uses the surface to show grain measures, butter paddles, an old bucket and an early kerosene lantern. Lisa made the pumpkin penny rug on top.

Lisa painted the original cupboards with Old Village 'Soldier Blue'. A graduated collection of brown manganese crocks holds staples below. Lisa added the small suspended shelf to provide an area for displaying her early tin spice containers.

Another shelf holds vintage tin above a matching reproduction breadbox with a punched tin front.

Vintage blue banded yellowware bowls are perfect above the blue cabinets. A mustard home spun curtain hides the oven.

Pumpkin Stew

2 lbs of 1" cubes stew meat

1 lg green pepper, chopped

3T vegetable oil, divided

4 garlic cloves, minced

1 Cup of water

1 medium chopped onion

3 lg peeled potatoes, cubed

2 teaspoons of salt

4 medium carrots, sliced

1 teaspoon of pepper

1 can (14 ½ oz) diced tomatoes

4 beef bouillon cubes

1 pumpkin (10-12 pounds), wash, remove seeds and loose fibers from inside

In a Dutch oven, brown meat in 2T of oil. Add water, potatoes, carrots, green peppers, garlic, onion, salt and pepper. Cover and simmer for 2 hours. Stir in bouillon and tomatoes. Place pumpkin in a sturdy shallow baking pan. Spoon stew into pumpkin and replace the top. Brush outside of pumpkin with remaining 1T of oil. Bake at 325° F for 2 hours or just until pumpkin is tender. Do not over-bake or your pumpkin may collapse. Serve stew from pumpkin scooping out a little pumpkin with each serving. Makes 8-10 servings and is great with crusty French bread.

The interior of the buttery is painted with Benjamin Moore 'Greenfield Pumpkin'. Lisa loves to collect barrels as they are not only relatively easy to find but the price is often right.

Lisa found the butter churn at a shop where it was being sold for parts. It had been marked down to $12 simply because it was missing the leg and cover – a piece of cake for Lisa to remedy!

Lisa made the hanging branch herb dryer with a sapling root from the yard. She enlisted the help of her children to peel off the bark to make various branch hooks for which they were able to earn $2.00 a hook!

Above the mantel in the living room, Lisa has hung a portrait of an unknown sitter. Lisa is anxiously waiting to replace this one with an actual family portrait offered to her by her grandmother.

Lisa built the mantel surround and who would have ever guessed it provides storage space for CD's and DVD's.

Lisa made the game board on the wall and used the rungs of an early ladder to exhibit textiles.

The mustard corner cupboard painted with Old Village 'Pearwood' was built using old doors. Lisa appreciates the fact that Leon often brings home something which he might initially think is worthless but knows Lisa will create something wonderful with it.

Lisa made the cupboard which hangs over an early bookcase she fondly calls the 'shoe shelf' where the children stored their boots and shoes when she operated the daycare center..

Lisa enjoys adding vintage doilies and often stains them with coffee to give them an earlier appearance.

Using old shutters found at the side of the road, Lisa built the cupboard seen right which holds stoneware crocks. The wall is painted with the same 'Greenfield Pumpkin' as the interior of the buttery.

The small wall cupboard in the back hallway leading to the combination bathroom and laundry room hides the thermostat. Below it, another roadside find has been painted to match.

Curtains conceal the washer and dryer. The entire room has been decorated with vintage laundry items such as rug beaters, towel racks, scrub boards, laundry baskets and early medicine bottles.

Lisa hung a tea-dyed muslin curtain over the cupboard which holds the bath linens. Above the toilet, an early tin grain scoop creates an ideal candleholder.

The wooden board beside the scoop is the side of an old crate with the lettering 'Sawyer's Crystal Blue'; below it stands an old bottle which originally held the same product!

Lisa drilled holes in the end of the JC Penny four-poster bed and threaded rope to make the bed look more period. She made the trundle bed beneath and found the wonderful 19thC baby cradle in original blue paint at Homestead Primitives.

Lisa has found many pieces of vintage clothing and enjoys displaying them, wherever there is space, on old racks.

Lisa creatively patterned the closet doors after early barn doors using plywood and overlaying tongue and groove planks.

In addition to building furniture, Lisa loves to sew and utilizes one room for storing her sewing notions. The bed is a 19thC three-quarter bed which Lisa has outfitted with a futon mattress and feather tick top.

The trestle table was purchased at The Country Mischief and Lisa has married it with a sorting cubby on top in which she stores her sewing 'gadgets'.

On the other side of the room, Lisa turned an early box on its side to create a shelf for crocks and other collectibles.

The original deck overlooks a pool. Lisa painted the shed to look more in keeping with the overall country feeling of the house.

While Lisa's creativity is exhibited inside the home, Leon's talents are showcased outside. He used three old ladders to build an arbor and in doing so connected two smaller garden areas. In addition to clearing the land, Leon built all the stone walls.

Lisa hasn't decided what to plant around the base of the glass mini greenhouse that Leon created using old window frames.

Since they have agreed they are not about to put more additions on the house, Leon and Lisa plan to direct their creativity to the grounds. They hope to replace the deck and shed with a stone patio area complete with outdoor fireplace, seating and hot tub OR build a 'work room' where they can each store tools and Lisa can continue to build. And of course . . . it goes without saying . . . the structure will have to look like an old barn!

Chapter 8

❤

Scott and Lorrie Fulton-Fowler

In 2005 Lorrie Fulton-Fowler put an addition on the back of the home in Deepwater, New Jersey where she and Scott live. The addition more than doubled the size giving Lorrie that much more space to fill with primitives. Lorrie, like many of us, seems to have recognized a love of decorating and appreciation for country at an early age. She admitted that although her mother was not into decorating, Lorrie was rearranging furniture when she was 10 years old. She enjoys the warm and comfortable feeling of primitives and soothing tones of browns and reds. Lorrie also benefits from her job at *Leighton's Olde Towne Shoppe*, a country antique shop in nearby Woodstown. There she is able to acquire many pieces when they are first available and in fact was able to purchase all of the upholstered furniture in the living room and family room from Denise, the owner of *Leighton's*.

Scott is 'not into country in any shape or form', according to Lorrie who further added, 'as long as he has his recliner and TV, he's happy'! Scott works as a rancher at the *Cowtown Rodeo* in Woodstown and prefers to spend what free time he has providing the muscle in the yard rather than accompanying Lorrie to flea markets.

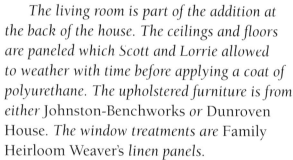

The living room is part of the addition at the back of the house. The ceilings and floors are paneled which Scott and Lorrie allowed to weather with time before applying a coat of polyurethane. The upholstered furniture is from either Johnston-Benchworks or Dunroven House. The window treatments are Family Heirloom Weaver's linen panels.

Lorrie found the Spanish Brown cupboard in Salem, New Jersey at Market Street Treasures. The shelves are filled with stoneware crocks, many with scratches or chips hidden in the back as Lorrie confessed she is not a purist and has no trouble paying less for a slightly flawed piece.

The small barrel resting on a make-do stand originally intended to hold a doughbox was found at Leighton's. The small keg in red paint on the floor was purportedly used to hold dynamite. The differential in sizes of the three kegs makes a nice grouping.

Lorrie also found the pie safe with brown paint at Market Street Treasures. The drop leaf table had already been repurposed as a coffee table when Lorrie acquired it.

The large 19thC platform horse was another Leighton's find. The original surface has been exposed and appears to be of a paper mache composition. The brown surface blends beautifully with those tones she likes best.

Lorrie uses the unique sized grain bin in oxblood red paint to hold the recyclables. A large cutting board with aged patina softens the corner above. The ladderback was a yard sale find for $5; the dough bowl on top is filled with yarn balls of fall colors.

Lorrie cut strips from an old piece of linen to make the tie backs for the window treatments

Lorrie has a passion for tables and chairs and loves to place two side by side! The table in the foreground was made by Primitiques; the second table is a sawbuck which Lorrie purchased at Leighton's. The chandelier was made by Carriage House Lighting in Troy, Ohio. The steps behind the table lead to the finished basement and family room. The kitchen which is between the dining room and living room area can be seen in the background .

Lorrie placed an early tool carrier on top of the green painted jelly cupboard; the ladderback chair holding a large gourd and bittersweet vines dress the piece for the season.

Lorrie purchased the bowl rack from Hidden Den in Ohio. Bowls, baskets and crocks are a few of her weaknesses!

Primitiques *made the make-do chair at the* end of the table. The bow back chairs are by Lawrence Crouse.

Lorrie chose to paint the kitchen cabinets with a paint from The Seraph *called 'Earth'.* She painted the wood countertops and applied polyurethane for protection.

An early cutting board covers the sink and holds one of the hand-poured Luminara candles from Marsh Homestead Country Antiques. The green slant top desk is early and fits perfectly under the cabinet above. A set of graduated fly screens is displayed on the side of the cupboard.

An early child's high chair with wonderful blue paint holds one of Arnett's Country Store bears.

Lorrie found the master bedroom bed advertised in the back of an early Country Sampler Magazine. She and Scott removed the wall to wall carpeting in the bedroom, part of the original house, and chose to expose the natural floors.

The bed linens are from Family Heirloom Weavers – a brown blanket with a brown grid throw over top.

What appears to be a small writing desk is actually an early tool box from an Amish buggy which Lorrie had Scott attach to the wall. A pair of glass bottles found in the backyard when Scott and Lorrie were digging to build a small pond stands on top. The bowback chair is from Lawrence Crouse.

The walking wheel at the foot of the bed was found at Leighton's. The trim paint in the room is Old Village 'Pearwood'.

Lorrie had just started to collect brooms prior to filming her home and was drawn to the brooms as the tones blend beautifully with the browns and neutral colors she favors. The whisk brooms on the door have some age while the others in the early measure sitting on the bench are newly crafted.

The basement is finished and not only offers Lorrie more space to decorate but Scott a place to enjoy his recliner and television. The couch, shown below left, is from Johnston-Benchworks; the make-do chair was made by Primitiques. A large cheese strainer hangs on the wall behind it. Lorrie used an old brown cradle on the coffee table to hold an arrangement of gourds.

A large early wooden section from a grain funnel, shown above right, holds a fall wreath and bittersweet. A 19thC lidded dough box with red paint stands on a bench beneath.

Beside a red painted bowback chair, an early piece of farm equipment, used to separate kernels from the ears of corn, is filled with gourds and dried corn husks.

Lorrie filled a large 19thC cradle with vintage red and white folded quilts and bears – two of which were made by Arnett's.

Lorrie couldn't resist placing two more tables end to end making the space large enough to hold a cradle of large dough bowls and at the far end a bowl of hog scrapers

An antique horse on glider shows signs of being well loved! It is most likely a 19thC child's toy which is straw stuffed and covered with burlap to 'extend its life'.

Lorrie placed two cutting boards on top of a 19thC slant top grain bin with original green paint; that way it not only provides a surface for the large gathering basket but looks more finished to Lorrie's eye.

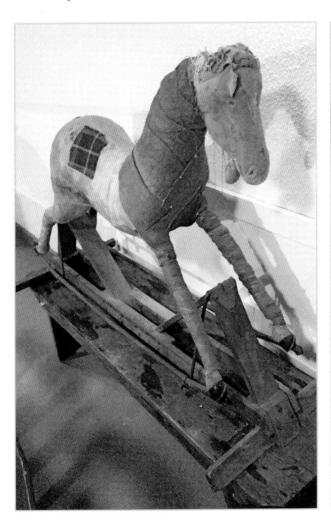

The early cupboard with red wash holds a television as well as an early toolbox with paint and basket on top.

Another 19thC jelly cupboard with original Spanish Brown paint holds manganese jugs on top and stoneware inside.

Lorrie and Scott enjoy the privacy of their backyard enclosed with stockade fence. They maintain a number of flower, vegetable and herb gardens and also stock their pond in the back with goldfish and Koi.

While Lorrie enjoys the personal contact with the customers at Leighton's Olde Towne Shoppe and welcomes the exchange of ideas she gleans from talking with them, she also loves the comfort of the home she and Scott have created. So much so that, if given the choice, Lorrie confessed she would rather be at home than take a vacation!

Chapter 9

❧ ✿ ☙

Tim and Kathy Hoehn

Tim and Kathy Hoehn have lived in their Lima, Ohio home since 1983. The house was built in 1980 and several years ago, Tim and Kathy built an addition on the back to include a screen porch that Kathy could not only enjoy while taking a break from gardening but also to provide another room to decorate.

Tim is a human resources supervisor with Husky Engineering Company, a local oil refinery. Kathy is a registered nurse who worked most recently as a non-traditional nurse aiding those with mental health issues and drug addicted families.

Kathy views herself as a leader rather than follower when it comes to decorating, as she was been decorating in a country style before it was in vogue and has always wanted her décor to look different. Initially Kathy, who has been a collector for over 30 years, was drawn to the style because it was a cost-effective way to furnish a home, recalling the days when it was possible to find a nice antique kitchen table for $50. She now enjoys mixing reproductions with antiques pieces and especially cherishes the few antiques she has which are family pieces passed down to her.

Tim 'goes with the flow' according to Kathy but does question 'when will it stop'! Of course as we all agree, none of us wants it to ever stop! Tim supports Kathy's passion for country though and goes along on the hunt. He is most interested in the historical aspect of the antiques.

Kathy lives just a few miles from a farm which sells gourds, pumpkins and mums that she often displayed with primitive pieces adding to the charm while providing Kathy with fresh ideas.

The entranceway of the house can accommodate many large pieces of furniture. The wingback chair was purchased in Findlay, Ohio at *Early American Home* where Kathy has found many of her favorite pieces. A wonderful assortment of early painted buckets fills the primitive bucket bench.

Mike Spangler created many of Kathy's pieces; one such piece is the rope bed. He can be found on Facebook.

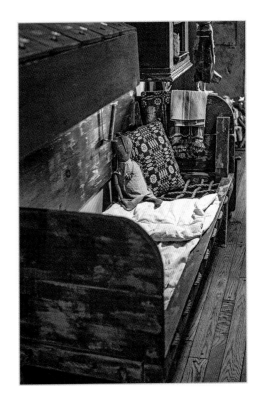

Kathy collects early tin lanterns; many of these are found at Eastman's Antiques, *a shop in* Mt. Victory Ohio. *The small slant top grain box was purchased from* Good Old Days *in Pultneyville, New York.*

The black jacket is an authentic Amish textile. The make-do corn husk broom was made by Cabin Creek 1812 *and purchased online.*

Mike Spangler made the hanging red cupboard with tin paneled door. The hanging iron ratchet candleholder is a reproduction.

Mike also made the small hanging red cupboard with the screen door. The sheep pull toy is a newly crafted piece. The hand poured grungy Luminara candle on the first shelf is from Marsh Homestead Antiques.

An early German platform horse is seen in the foreground in the living room. Kathy found the horse at Eastman's. The 19thC six-board blanket chest was one purchase Kathy made with 'fun money' she earned teaching childbirth classes to private clients. The jack-o-lantern is a paper mache vintage collectible. One of Kathy's favorite pieces, the early blue carrier, stands on top of the long dry sink which most likely originated as a storage piece in a general store.

Mike Spangler also made the primitive make-do bowl holder on the riser atop the coffee table.

Kathy purchased the couch from a local shop as she was drawn to the blue tones and the pattern of the fabric.

When Kathy purchased the paneled cupboard in the corner it was a bright oak piece but the doors appealed to her for their uniqueness. Kathy used Caromal Colours and painted the cupboard 'Peppercorn' adding extra toner to darken it. The make-do chair was a gift to Kathy from her daughter.

The box in the center of the mantel is from *Primitiques* and is referred to as a 'remedy box'. Kathy keeps some of her miniature snowman collection out all year long in the chimney cupboard.

Kathy purchased the sawbuck table at the now closed shop, The Shaker Shed. The bowback chair is a reproduction; the ladder back is early. The floor cloth is from *Primitiques*.

A graduated set of pantry boxes, found at Eastman's, stands on the seat of a black settle made by *Primitiques*. Kathy draped a latch hook rug on the back to add color and more texture.

The blue cupboard in the back corner is 19thC and was found at The Shaker Shed.

Kathy is partial to early blue paint and the vibrant blue of the box on the riser made it a must-have.

The desk on top is from Primitiques. The painted pantry boxes are reproductions.

The large walnut cupboard holds special meaning to Kathy as it belonged to her great-great-great grandfather. The early treen candleholder is an Eastman's find. The shelves are filled with boxes, early mortars and pestles, baskets and in front a pipe box with clay pipes.

The kitchen floor is quarry tiles. Kathy painted the kitchen cabinets with a Caromal Colours color named 'Pumpkin'.

A farrier's carrier holds a blue painted bowl on the shelf of a dry sink crafted by Primitiques. A hand-poured Luminara grungy candle by Marsh Homestead Antiques stands in front.

The work table with original mustard paint was found at The Shaker Shed. *The lollipop spoon rack in red wash is from* Primitiques. *The riser was crafted by* Lizzie's Cabin Primitives *in Ohio. The hanging cupboard with dry gray paint is from* Early American Home. *Kathy uses the open space for showing measures, hand hewn bowls and a match holder.*

At one end of the kitchen, the small early square table fits perfectly in the space for a dining nook. The table retains original paint on the base and legs. The make-do wing chair in the back is from Early American Home *and the ladderback chairs are from* Primitiques.

The open stepback is a married piece; the base retains original red paint. The top holds many treen early painted pieces and some of Kathy's redware collection. A newly-crafted burlap pumpkin appliquéd sack holds dried Sweet Annie.

The coverlet on the master bedroom bed is from Family Heirloom Weavers. The black cupboard below is from Primitiques and is called a 'sister cupboard'; the blue cupboard, also from Primitiques, is called a document cupboard as it would have been used to conceal valuable papers.

Kathy created shutters in the bathroom from stained glass panels. The apothecary on the counter and the small red cupboard seen right are both from Primitiques.

Make-do bath accessories such as a shaving mirror and early toothbrush, made by Lizzie's Cabin, complement the 'soap on a rope' on the vanity.

The doorway seen left opens to the screened porch area which Tim and Kathy's grandchildren refer to as 'Basil's Room' – the hired man's room!

Kathy feels that country decorating is an outlet for those of us with a creative spirit. The fact that a rope bed, made by Mike Spangler, in the screen porch belongs to an imaginary occupant by the name of Basil, adds some humor. The child's rocker with original blue green paint is early.

The wing back chair is upholstered with early feed sacks. The dry sink behind it is from Primitiques. Kathy had it plumbed so she has running water in the room.

Kathy's decorating doesn't end with the inside of the house but continues around the entire side and backyard.

The potting shed was built with old barn floor boards. Kathy loves to garden but also enjoys using the potting shed for other country decorating.

Tim and Kathy have tried to instill in their children and grandchildren a strong sense of history using the various antiques as examples. Their hope is that their curiosity has been piqued despite the fear by Kathy that when she and Tim are gone, the kids might board the doors to the house shut!

Chapter 10

❧ ✽ ❧

Fred and Nina Meacham

Fred and Nina Meacham's Canal Winchester, Ohio home was built in 1990 but the fine detail used by the previous owner makes the house appear to have been built centuries earlier. Fred and Nina even 'inherited' the boxwood gardens consisting of over 120 boxwoods which Fred meticulously maintains.

The house is sided with cedar and the roof is a unique metal Shaker style. Fred and Nina purchased the house in 2009 when a realtor called Nina to let her know that the saltbox she had previously expressed an interest in was available. Nina had no intention of moving again and at the time had a cottage on a lake but admits she was just nosy enough that she told the realtor she would take a look. We know how that went!

Fred is retired from the Kroger Company, a large grocery store chain and Nina retired from her position as a secretary for a masonry contractor. Just prior to her retirement, the owner of the company, for whom she had the utmost respect, presented Nina with the farm wagon seen left on Secretary's Day. When the owner was killed in a tragic accident not long after, Nina vowed that wherever she moved, the wagon was going with her.

Nina comes by her love of country naturally as her parents were both avid collectors and she grew up surrounded with the look she now embraces in their home. Nina's sister received many of their parent's antiques and upgraded from quality reproductions at that time. Nina was able to purchase selected reproductions from her sister.

The red-checkered couch in the living room is a Johnston-Benchworks piece. Nina purchased the wonderful 19thC six-board chest at a yard sale years ago for $7. On top stands a dough bowl filled with stone fruit and a small Shaker box.

The mustard cupboard at the back is a reproduction handcrafted by a folk artist from Chillicothe, Ohio. A large glass front cabinet in the corner holds a large collection of folded new and vintage quilts.

The blue work table is an antique and one of Nina's favorite pieces. Not only does she like the patina on the scrub top but the two drawers of different sizes which add character. A dough bowl on top holds a large gourd; a 19thC leather-bound dictionary is beside it.

Tucked in the corner, a slant top desk with original white paint was purchased from Linda Miller; it stands on a newly crafted custom-made base.

The open top stepback is a new piece crafted from old barn boards; it was made by The Barn in Ashville, Ohio. The sign above was painted by a friend on an old board. The bowls were purchased from Nina's sister.

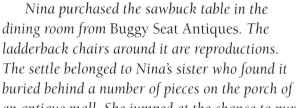

Nina purchased the sawbuck table in the dining room from Buggy Seat Antiques. The ladderback chairs around it are reproductions. The settle belonged to Nina's sister who found it buried behind a number of pieces on the porch of an antique mall. She jumped at the chance to purchase it for $65!

The whimsical tavern sign above has some age, according to Nina, but is a 21stC creation.

There are two fireplaces in the house both of which Fred and Nina converted to gas which helps them heat the house during the cold Ohio winters.

Interestingly, Nina purchased most of the Wilton pewter seen in the red reproduction cupboard from a woman in Lancaster, Ohio. As it turns out, the woman had purchased the collection from the previous owner of Fred and Nina's home.

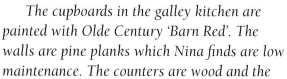

The cupboards in the galley kitchen are painted with Olde Century 'Barn Red'. The walls are pine planks which Nina finds are low maintenance. The counters are wood and the sink is a granite composition. Nina displays three faux loaves of bread in the vintage pie shelf on the blue painted jelly cupboard. Using an old door, Nina's sister made the hand-painted sign above.

The bed in this guestroom is an early rope bed; the linens are from Family Heirloom Weavers. Both cupboards are reproductions. A friend painted the hat sign over the headboard and Nina added an old top hat on the bed to tie it together.

The early desk belonged to Nina's parents.

Nina had the rope bed in the master bedroom painted a country blue. The doll chair belonged to Nina's father as a child; it holds a reproduction bear. On the opposite side of the blue painted chest, the red settle chair holds an Arnett's doll.

The large platform horse is a newly crafted piece acquired from Nina's sister.

Nina occasionally changes the use of the room originally intended as the dining room. The room is located immediately off the kitchen making it ideal for a cozy sitting room while keeping an eye on what's cooking in the kitchen.

Nina commissioned Sally Whims to paint the corner cabinet. The red jelly cupboard beside it is also a reproduction and holds a television.

Nina uses another small room off the kitchen as a buttery which she has staged with artificial fruits and vegetables. A black wood stove holds faux cakes and pastries.

In closing, Nina confessed that their homes had been featured in other publications over the years and that she has a habit of becoming bored with a home once it has been featured in a book or magazine! I asked if she was sure she wanted me to continue with her chapter! She replied that it was all right since she is confident she and Fred will stay where they are even after their house is featured in the August book! I guess we'll have to wait and see!

Chapter 11

Nelson and Kristen Baltazar

Nelson and Kristen Baltazar moved into their Old Wethersfield, Connecticut home 20 years ago and have been renovating, remodeling and redoing ever since. The result is spectacular! Each room is tastefully decorated with crafted furniture and folk art accessories. The trim colors vary in each room yet blend throughout as a visitor meanders from one room to the next in this 4000 square foot colonial nestled at the end of a quiet cul-de-sac. Kristen attributes her decorating style to her mother and the fact that she grew up surrounded with antiques. Her dad restored antique cars and she reminisces with fondness the car shows she attended. Even as a child, Kristen wanted to collect antiques and in fact still has a few of those first treasures. Nelson gives Kristen free rein with her decorating. He not only appreciates the home she has created but is happy to go antiquing and be the patient chauffer on her hunts.

Nelson is a global logistics executive and enjoys skiing and biking in his spare time. Kristen is a former fourth grade teacher and is now employed as a part-time math resource teacher allowing her time for her other passions; her family, gardening, baking, decorating, crafts and Nantucket! Kristen's love of Nantucket Island is evident as the house is 'peppered' throughout with mementos of the island where the family visits at least three times a year to enjoy the local events, shops and, of course, beaches.

The color of the vinyl siding is Woodland Green. The front door is painted with Old Village 'New England Red'. Kristen chose the boxwoods and topiaries as she likes the orderly effect they provide and wanted to pattern the landscaping after an English garden look. The hydrangeas on either side of the front steps were not in bloom but are usually full of blue blossoms.

Kristen chose the garden statue of a girl and boy amidst the hostas as it reminded her of their two children, Benjamin, 14, and Hanna, 9.

The living room is entered from the front door on the right side of the hallway and to the right. It also opens at the other side of the room to the rear of the house where the kitchen and family room span the back.

The mantel and trim are painted with 'New England Red'. The beluga whale was carved by folk artist Wick Ahrens and purchased at The Four Winds Craft Guild on Nantucket. A painting by Christopher Gurshin depicting historic Old Wethersfield Cove hangs on the lintel. A vintage basket is filled with dried hydrangea blooms in the fireplace; the yarn winder on the hearth is early.

Eldred Wheeler of Hanover, Massachusetts crafted the large tiger maple desk. The top shelf holds three vintage Nantucket baskets while the whale on the middle shelf is flanked by two more. On the lowest shelf a nest of baskets was made by Bill and Judy Sayles; the others on the shelf by Dale Rutherford. The scrimshaw is a reproduction piece found at the museum shop on Nantucket.

The sofa is from the Hitchcock factory in Riverton, Connecticut. The penny rug on the table, purchased at Old Saybrook Country Barn, is from Tessier's shop, Changes in Thyme. The wax pineapple in the center was made by Marsh Homestead Country Antiques. A ship print by Kolene Spicher hangs above the couch while the shelf over it holds a collection of antique baskets.

Nelson and Kristen purchased the shorebirds at the Farmington Antique Show. They stand on a mustard painted corner cupboard purchased at Americana Workshop in York, Maine.

Kristen filled the hanging cupboard found at the former American Heritage Shop in Kent, Connecticut. Early sewing baskets, old books and bird nests blown from trees and picked up during Kristen's morning walks line the shelves.

A stack of graduated Nantucket baskets, won in a phone auction, is silhouetted against the front window. The bear beside it sits on a vintage bike Kristen purchased as a child.

The small stepback was made from old wood by Americana Workshop.

The writing comb back chair was made by Lawrence Crouse.

While Kristen's mother influenced her decorating style, Kristen's father's knowledge of antique pewter and his collections of same created an appreciation by Kristen for pewter.

Two prints by Kolene Spicher hang behind the chair. A small tiger maple splay-leg table crafted by Paul Rulli holds a special treasure. Nelson commissioned three Nantucket folk artists to make the Nantucket basket for Kristen as a gift. The sailor represents Nelson and carries a telescope with Nelson's initials.

The decoy on the shelf was purchased at Village Primitives in Sturbridge, Massachusetts. It hangs below a hydrangea wreath Kristen made.

The trim in the front hall is Old Village 'Cupboard Blue'. The reproduction mustard cupboard holds baskets, Barbara Stein pin cushions and basket of Stein fabric eggs.

The dining room walls are painted with a sweeping mural by Susan Dwyer, (www.susandwyerartwork. com) that depicts Old Wethersfield and representations of early schooners in the Cove as well as some of the early buildings.

The tiger maple table was made by J. L. Treharn and was purchased from The Keeping Room in Virginia. The reproduction chairs were found at The Seraph in Sturbridge. The hooked rug on the

center is from Tessier's Changes in Thyme as was most of the redware in the corner cupboard. The cupboard also holds a collection of antique and reproduction green glass

Three Maine early sap buckets stand on the bucket bench from Tessiers. In the corner, the small reproduction grandmother clock was crafted by Stephen Von Hohen and was purchased at Old Saybrook Country Barn.

Both the tiger maple table in the corner and graduated set of terra cotta pumpkins were found at The Seraph.

One section of the mural incorporates the Baltazar's home in the landscape.

The trim and panels below the chair rail are painted with Old Village 'Colonial Green'.

A small lavatory is found in the hallway leading to the back of the house. The small ironing board was one of the first antiques Kristen purchased.

An antique birdcage is seen on top of the small hanging cupboard purchased from Circa Home Living.

The trim is Old Village 'Valley Forge Mustard'.

The wax rabbit made from an early cast iron mold, seen right, was done by Marsh Homestead Country Antiques.

When Nelson and Kristen renovated the kitchen six years ago, Kristen didn't want 'kitchen clutter' on the counters so a door was

removed from the hall closet and converted into a built-in pantry.

The kitchen was custom-designed with hand-planed pine cupboards and slate countertops. The rug is a Karastan. The table was crafted by a local craftsman while the chairs are Lawrence Crouse.

The early dough bowl on the center of the table is filled with fruit crafted by Barbara Stein.

Kristen developed a love of antique German blue onionware from her mother who is also an avid collector. Various pieces fill the shelves and cupboards.

The floor cloth is by Michele Hollick of New Hampshire.

A reproduction cabinet from American Heritage is filled with blue onionware. How pretty the contrast is between the blue and white and black.

A stoneware salt-glazed batter jug purchased at Mad River Antiques is to the left of a unique blue onion pie crimper holder and set of six egg cups.

A faux bundt cake 'fresh from the oven' cools on the stove. The miniature cabinet was a gift from Nelson who commissioned their kitchen cabinetmaker to make the replica for Kristen after she lost her bid for one on eBay®. Kristen painted it to give it age and filled it with miniature crocks made by Jane Graber. The primitive snowman is a Jennifer Schneeman piece; the sampler above was wrought by Kristen.

An early yellowware rolling pin hangs above a cake crock given as a gift to Kristen by Nelson.

The small tree decorated with miniature gourds was purchased at the Walker Show in Brookfield, Massachusetts

Kristen used an antique French bread tray to display her blue onion rolling pin and faux pears. The print above is signed by Sharon Tremoureth.

The table in front of the window leading into the family room holds faux chocolates, bread and small bundt cakes.

The couch is from Angel House in Brookfield. The library table behind it was made with an old floor board for the top. The pin cushions were crafted by Barbara Stein and the pear by Schneeman. They were purchased in Bantam, Connecticut at Toll House Antiques.

The flame stitch chair is from The Seraph. A black shelf holds baskets and a large beeskep. The hooked wall hanging is from Changes in Thyme.

The swan over the mantel is from Circa Home Living. The pewter chargers and graduated set of measures on the mantel are all old. A hand-poured Luminara flameless candle made by Marsh Homestead Country Antiques stands at the end of the mantel. The dough bowl on the hearth is filled with gourds. Beside it is a large amber jug in which Kristen has placed a small strand of white lights on a timer which in the evening gives the fireplace a glow. Actually Kristen uses lights on timers throughout the inside and outside of their home and you'll hear me say more than once how she uses them to give a warm homey feeling to the rooms and yard.

The large tiger maple cupboard in the corner was made by J. L. Treharn; it houses a television. The writing desk is an antique. Sitting on the arm is an antique pewter inkwell Kristen couldn't resist as it is initialed 'K'. The swan decoy is new as is the small miniature six-board chest it stands on found at Tessiers.

The sun porch off the family room was added in 2006.

Kristen's dad made the glass greenhouse which is filled with starfish, shells, coral, blue marbles and, of course, tiny white lights on a timer which illuminates the glass house after dark giving the impression of everything being underwater.

A blue glass buoy is suspended from the window frame. Above it, a replica of a ship's masthead carved by Jack and Patricia Johnson was purchased from Three Point Design in Nantucket.

Kristen made the small tree decorated with shells. Kristen found the large mercury glass shells, gourds and pumpkins at Pottery Barn. They have a hole in the base to accommodate a string of small white lights – of course!

Kristen found the early wagon with original green paint at the Walker Homestead Show in Brookfield.

Walking back through the family room to the front hall, a display of early cutters is arranged on either side of the cellar door.

Kristen found the hooked rug pattern designed by Polly Minnick seen on the cover of my earlier book, The Spirit of Country. Kristen commissioned a folk artist to hook the rug substituting one of the male figures in the parade for a female so that both her son and daughter were represented.

A bucket bench from Tessier's shop stands at the top of the stairs in the hallway. The J. Porter sign above was done by Kathy Graybill.

Kristen adapted an idea from my earlier book, Of Hearth and Home, to add silhouettes of her children and their dog to the back stairway. She had an artist create the outline and using an overhead projector, projected the shape on the wall. Kristen then traced the shapes and painted the figures.

The landing at the top of the back stairs contains a bench with primitive animals and a cupboard from Tessier's filled with animals by Barbara Stein.

The large room to the right of the landing is called 'the bonus room'! And it sure is! It's huge and filled with comfortable furniture

The trim paint is Old Village 'Valley Forge Mustard'. Kristen had the large chair reupholstered at Angel House. The helping hands fabric box on the coffee table is from Changes in Thyme. A Claire Murray hooked rug of a schooner is in the foreground.

Wick Ahrens carved both the large sperm whale above the mantel and the smaller narwhal whale on the lintel.

Kristen used the antique desk to create what she likes to think of as a ship captain's desk with an early quill and hourglass. The window over the desk has bull's eye glass.

Folk artists Mo and Kelly Dallas of Good Book Folk Art in Ohio made the Noah's Ark and animals.

The painted chest, shown middle left, was purchased at Old Saybrook Country Barn.

Mo and Kelly Dallas created the Nantucket Sleigh Ride sign over the two windows.

A Kolene Spicher print of Brant Point Lighthouse in Nantucket hangs below another hydrangea wreath Kristen made.

An early goat cart with original green paint was found at Mad River Antiques. Kristen leaves the small tree up year round and of course at night the tiny lights illuminate.

The back stairs landing hallway connects to the hall in the main section of the house. A local craftsman built the open cupboard in which Kristen displays redware and yelloware. Kathy Graybill made the redware sign.

Kristen made the clay pipe on the tiger maple table at the end of the main hall. She used 'sculpy clay' found at Michaels craft store.

Susan Dwyer painted the mural at the end of the hall. The ship model seems in place with the backdrop of Nantucket waters. The saltbox represents the Jethro Coffin house – the oldest house on the island.

The guestroom is the former master bedroom. The bed was made by Eldred Wheeler and the coverlets are Family Heirloom Weavers.

The cradle is the first antique Kristen purchased. It holds early dolls; the middle one was made for Kristen as a child by her mother.

The slant front desk belonged to Kristen as a child. Above is a display of reproduction wallpaper boxes.

The guest bath is elegant with a large glass door shower and granite vanity top.

Susan Dwyer continued the Nantucket mural up the staircase to the master bedroom on the third floor. Two lighthouses are shown – one the Brant Point Lighthouse.

The trim in the master bedroom is a custom-mixed sage green. The tiger maple bed was made by Eldred Wheeler. Kristen made the lamps on either side of the bed from old amber glass bottles.

The headboard resembles waves or to my eye, whale tales, but in the center Wheeler added a raised Nantucket basket carving. Kristen made the sampler.

Tucked in the corner, Kristen's dad made the small shelf which holds an antique sewing basket, hourglass and hand-poured Luminara candle by Marsh Homestead Country Antiques.

The rug is a Karastan piece. Jennifer Schneeman made the fabric pear on the Wheeler crafted desk.

The fireplace is gas. The portrait of a ship's captain was purchased at Circa Home Living as was the small wall shelf which holds candle snuffers. The whale carving is another by Wick Ahrens. Kristen found the painting on board in Nantucket. It was found in a house in Siasconset, a village at the eastern end of Nantucket. The chairs are from Angel House.

The bureau is called a block and shell chest. It is made of tiger maple and was crafted by Wheeler.

Holding a place of honor in the room is a Christmas gift from Nelson to Kristen – a Jose Reyes original Nantucket purse.

Kristen commissioned Kathy Graybill to paint the sign to give the master bedroom the feeling of a room at the Nantucket Hotel.

The master bath is painted with 'Linen Gray' by Sherwin-Williams. The countertops are Carrera marble. The vertical gray panel at the right side of the picture above is a fold-out ironing board complete with the iron and a concealed electrical outlet. Rick Brown of Dreamworks, the contractor for the third floor project, designed all of the panels in the room as doors to open for additional storage space.

The deck in back is entered from the sun porch or the kitchen. Kristen blended a shell water fountain and birdbath to provide a soothing trickle heard from the porch.

Kristen loves to garden and her job affords her the opportunity in the summer when schools are closed.

The potting shed features a country appeal with gourds and a small cupola.

Kristen particularly likes flowers which would have traditionally been found in an English garden such as hollyhocks, fairy roses and fox gloves. Oh . . . I forgot to mention all the fences and trellis are strung with tiny white lights so at dusk they are programmed to go on and create a fairy garden.

Kristen purchased the large volcanic rock shells at Stonewall Kitchen.

When the third floor master bedroom was completed, Nelson asked Kristen "Are we done now?" With seemingly no more space to renovate or remodel that I could see, I suggested perhaps it was time to look for property on Nantucket and save on all those ferry fees. That way Kristen could start with a fresh palette. 'Hmm' . . . she said, 'We'll have to think about that.'